To you —y

# Grey Love
**by Jason Shelley**

By the same author
**No Looking Back**

Grey Love

First published in 2003 by
**Tlön Books Publishing Ltd**
London SE1 6TE

Typography by **Ravi Chandwani**
Front cover and illustration by **Vishal Shah**

ISBN 0954146816

Printed and bound in Great Britain
by **Aldgate Press Ltd**, London E1

A CIP record for this book Is available from
the British Library

## Jack talks about the cold weather

It is about 6pm. I don't know what is wrong with me at times like these. Why on Earth I stayed in today, I do not know. Well, I didn't stay in, I went to the supermarket. That was a trip I was pleased with. Suddenly, I feel many things crashing down on my head. I'm thinking I have to pay back my debts. The time I pay back what I pay out each month would be a great time. I'm here with a packet of frozen peas on my knee, with a table full of books, feeling sorry for myself. The books are my books, written by me and assembled by me.

Why might I feel sorry for myself? Well the two closest people I know, did not telephone me when they said they would. Is it too much for someone to do, to do something they said they'd do? - telephone. It isn't too much too ask.

Those great writers were good because they could look at a place and say to themselves, this is the right kind of place. They could set up a couple of characters then write about the place.

I've got a place. It has just one bedroom, a kitchen, a bathroom and a lounge. A place, all mine. All mine, ready to worry about repayments, about the walls falling down. I'd worry about how to decorate it. Maybe someone could live there with me.

I had a severe headache, earlier. I'm feeling much better. I'm writing with a clearer head. I still feel sick. The tea I'm drinking could come back at any time.

The good thing about me is that I feel settled. I feel settled enough to write. I don't know why that is. It might have something to do with a conversation with my bank manager, yesterday. It might have something to do with that.

More likely, it might have something to do with making a breakthrough last night. I sat down and tapped away on my computer. I was putting together something that looked to be the start of a novel. Problem was that that outburst, last night, led to the start of my terrible headache, today. What had happened was that I had looked at a computer screen too late at night.

## Jack, late February, early March

The cold man is very, very cold. For some reason she is feeling very, very guilty about what is going on. That isn't all that good at all. I suppose what we're doing is going down to Cornwall for a weekend, which is okay. But we're not going, now. Unfortunately not. The severe feeling of guilt she has is overwhelming. The way I'm feeling now is good. I feel as though I can fill one page after another with good stuff after good stuff. And it is all because I don't have anyone. I have got someone. She is a woman unhappy with her life.

It is difficult to work out exactly what I am supposed to be doing. I mean with writing, that is. The last few years have consisted of a spell of desperation.

**9/4/03**

Got a bit of a headache today. I came up with a good title yesterday/last night (which was connected to what I said to her about watching trash t.v.). I think that definitely would make a good title for the book. It is neccessary now, to go ahead and make the damn thing. Then make another one. I have big problems with writing, on a daily basis. Often I think, gosh you are a small fellow (I should use that in my favour. Perhaps have a little fight with the rest of the world).

I think that person we're thinking about is okay but I don't want to spend all my fighting time making her like me. I don't want that to be the way things are. I find that what is motivating her in her life is that feeling she has, that there is an urgency to

**25th July 2000 Tuesday**
**Jason Shelley writing as Jason Shelley**
**London Bridge**
Dear nobody

I am on the train to Brighton. The train is an express. It stops first at Croydon, then goes all the way to Brighton. It also stops at Gatwick.

There is a nun sitting opposite me. If she weren't doing what I'm going to tell you she is doing, I wouldn't have mentioned her. She is eating an apple with a knife and a paper napkin which she has on her lap. My first thoughts when I saw her do this were, if I were her I wouldn't need a knife and napkin. I would gobble up the apple with my hand and mouth.

I bought my ticket at London Bridge. I was lucky to find my train left at 12.40pm from platform 5. I had finished buying my ticket at 12.36. That left me a comfortable 4 minutes to get to the platform. To tell you the truth, I feel rotten again. I feel run down. I felt like this before I flew to Athens. There, it took me a whole week to shake off a strange virus.

I tend to pick up this virus if I spend too much time on my own. When I have company that I like, I am fine. This company that I mention, is people that are similar to myself. They are struggling, poverty stricken people. If I am with a successful person I feel uncomfortable. I suppose all people feel good with people they have things in common with.

The virus takes me by surprise me. It takes me down. When I have it, all things can get to me. I think I am a failure for one reason, or the other; I have no strength to defend myself when under attack. I get aches and pains until something good happens. When that happens the aches and pains go away.

On the way to the train station, I came up with a conclusion about myself. When I thought of it, I knew I wanted to make a note of it when I got on the train. I know what causes my falling. It happened the same at Paul's apartment, when I stayed there at Christmas time. It is staring into the air, it is nothing; having no social interactions, no other stimulation. I'm not sure that I got it in my flat in Stockwell (there I had painted my flat yellow). There I got a different kind of bad depression.

I felt worse and worse, last night, on my own. I attempted to salvage myself. It couldn't be done. My body had no energy. It got to a point where all I could do was slump back into that body. By that time, at 11.30pm, I got a call. It was a wrong number. The person on the other line didn't speak, but I knew it was a wrong number, it must have been.

I called it back. No connection. I rang the number six more times. The sixth time the 6th time I connected. Hello, hello, I said. No reply. That person wasn't paying for the call. Therefore they could have stayed on the line forever and ever. I thought I could hear the person breathing. I could definitely hear the t.v. The sound was faint, in the background. I wanted to get out of my bed, turn my t.v. on and see what channel they were watching. I couldn't be bothered. Instead I disconnected the call and sent a text message, which she or he replied to. He or she said, who r u then? To this I gave not an answer but three questions, to which they did not respond.

I've had no calls or texts since.

The nun next to me peeled her apple and ate it. She carefully put aside the core and the skin.

As I was saying, I fall down. I'm almost dead. The call from the secret person almost revived me. There wasn't anybody talking on the other end. I need to have things in my life that give me energy, that stop me from falling down. I know I shouldn't stay in my flat, alone. In Paul's place I'd sit facing the wall, facing nothing. I'd sink. I should go out at lunchtimes. Should go out to literary lunches at the Savoy. Should get myself out of it. Have a break, come back, have a break, come back?

The leg is getting better. Walworth Road is a downright pigsty. I'll speak to Ülku, from the Turkish supermarket. We'll take breaks together, sometime soon.

## Watching t.v. and other stuff

I have a strong desire to break that window, over there. I want to break it big time.

I don't know what was going on, yesterday, at my brother's house.

Now, and for a long time, I'll write down a lot. It was a terrible day yesterday. Yesterday was terrible. Today, I feel surprisingly calm which is strange. I know that I am not going out with any other young people. Why that is I do not know. I've got to get out with my mates and do things. My brother goes out with people from his work but doesn't call me. When he had his last day that time, that was very odd. Now, he has a 36" Sony t.v. life is also very odd. For some reason things are running away without us. Things are running away. There isn't much we can do about that except get up go to work, do all the other things we do, like pick up the post and a number of other things I won't mention now.

Yesterday, I received a great deal of discouragement. The discouragement I received did not make me feel happy. I liked it at my brother's house. My brother and his wife put their bottles of wine on the table. We drank the wine, then cleared up.

Christine went and sat over the park, yesterday. She got annoyed because the people playing cricket kept whacking the cricket ball over near her, which made her leave.

If my leg wasn't killing me I could do a whole lot more stuff.

**Iceland**

Outside. Three people.
Old lady speaking to younger lady looking after
Man with mental disability.
Man is smacked around head by
Lady looking after him.
Older lady looks one quarter shocked.

I go into Iceland.
I buy my shopping.
At back of checkout
Small child in pram
Throws his red mittens at my feet.
I pick them up and give them back.

**by the sea**
Her walking out into the night scratching her head.
Her riding her bike.
The wrench.
The dislocation.
The breaking.
The cruelty.
The destruction.
The pulling apart.
The looking back, the sadness.

**tomorrow**
I'll have no money to spend tomorrow.
It will be cold.
I can go to my flat.
If I stay there I'll get depressed.

I can look at the buses.
I won't catch a bus.
Buses cost money.
I can look at the people.
I can fall asleep.

### urban life

Blue, black hair.
Piercing.
Pale face.
Pale skin.
We go to the chip shop.
We buy fish and chips
And share it.

We watch our pennies.
We have homes.
We pay rent.

**grumpy**
This morning she observed her ankle;
She compared it to her other ankle.
She did this in bed.

She lifted her ankles into the air.

I looked at her ankles and her legs.

For a few brief moments she held them in the air.
Then she put them back under the covers.

**untitled**

Billy calls me from downstairs.

Jason, he says.

It is Judith on the phone. I act to go down.

I make it clear that I am on my mobile phone.

He says, I'll tell her you'll call her back.

I call her back as soon as I can.

The call is better than I expect.

She took a while to answer.

She is in the bath.

She says, can she call me back.

She calls me back.

She says she was wet when I called.

I grab a stall.

I sit down. The call is better than I expect.

Billy says bye.

He is studying.

He goes.

I talk.

She smokes a cigarette.

She doesn't like the new shelf put in her kitchen.

It seems we're hooked.

**i don't care**

Get rid of it. Calm yourself. Don't freak out.

Get rid of that stuff that makes you nervous, that makes your head throb, your face pale, that makes you look frightening,

And people think, look there is another mad man on the streets not knowing what to do with himself.

It is as simple as this.

Now I am going out. I am buying a sandwich from the Seven Eleven to eat. I am hungry. My body will take it in like a metal dustbin.

## what is underneath the celebrity

We get a bus in the morning,
monday morning.
She is going to work.

"It takes too long," she says.
"It only took twenty minutes from where I was before."
"More back then." I said.
She laughs.

"When I have to come in to work for my eight o'clock shift, there'll
be more traffic than this."
I tell her there won't be.

"The cat messed by the door," she said.
She says that because she's trying to find reasons why she shouldn't
have moved in.

We get near to her work. She buys some breakfast. Do you want
some, she says.  I say no. She gets to work dead on time.

**thursday**

In the evening I met a girl I know in the French House.

She invited me to her house. I went there.

She offered me some Red Stripe which I didn't want. Instead I had coffee.

We stayed up late listening to music. She was a musician.

She offered me a smoke.

I didn't smoke anything because I had to get up for work in the morning.

### sea

There is no point in imagining the sea.
I have seen it.
I know what it is like.
I don't want to go and see it again.
Not at the moment, anyway.

**Airport observation**
Men on their own are creepy.
Women on their own are creepy.
If they stare at somebody when not on their own that is not creepy.
Men and women can feel insecure on their own.

## People on their own
There is a certain performance
Or style, involved in being
On your own in public places.

**untitled**
**a. First thoughts on the aeroplane**
To make it as a writer
Would mean I'd be lonely.
Being a writer would be
Lonely and thrilling.

**b. Overheard conversation**
One air stewardess said
To the other that she
Wanted to get back
Quickly so she could go
To sleep.

**c. Last Part of Flight to Athens**
Once you've been on
Holiday for a week and
You are taking a flight
Marking the beginning
Of the second you
Start thinking less about
what you do at work
And, more how important your
Work is. In conversation
You listen well to what
Other people do.

**Films, nowadays**
They're always about
Desperate circumstances.
Things are not always
Like that.
He says sitting in the
Airport of his holiday
Destination.

**silent sunset**
Sun is low above
Mountains on horizon.
Occasional car passes
In background.
Hear birds and an aeroplane.
Water silent but for the
Quiet ripple every second.
An ant on my hand.
I pick up a rock and
Throw it into the water.
It breaks the silence.

**11am**
Coat.
Sun.
Eyes shut.
Balcony.
Sea breeze.
Distant sounds.
Chatter.
Scooters.
Children in school playground.

## Untitled

Once you get yourself into a certain state i.e. low, lonely, it is very
difficult to get yourself out of it.
If you are living in winter time, and you
Travel somewhere with sun;
If you are on your own, you'd look at your beard,
Or your hair, overgrown and lifeless.
If you feel like that,
Not even the clearest sunset, over
the clearest mountainside
Can pull you out of it.

**Heavy Rain**
Sunday, it is.
At the bus stop it was
Pelting it down.
I've never seen it
Rain so much.

I waited for a
Bus.
The next one to come happened to be a 176.
I got on it with a few other people.
The windows were steamed up,
So you couldn't see much.

I was looking forward to the end of the journey.

**local supermarket**
Enter shop. Looking at orange juice.
"Jason. Jason." I turn round.
I walk to checkout. "Hello."
Her mobile rings. She switches it off.
A customer in front
of me, with water
melon, wanting something
else; who leaves. "What are you doing
tonight," I say. I want to ask
her out.
"I don't finish until 11," she
says, "so I'm not doing anything. I'm
going clubbing tomorrow night."
Silence.
"I've got the day off
tomorrow." I say.
"What are you doing?" she says.
Silence.
I shrug
my shoulders. "I'm just hanging out."
"Are you going out with your
friends?" she says.
I nod. She says, "Where do you go out?"
Silence.
"I've just moved to the area. I don't know
where to go out." I say.
Silence.
"Okay. See
you later then," she says.

**woman**
Woman in street
Asks for money.
I give her 20p.

She hides her eyes with the tip of her baseball cap.
I say have a nice day.
She says she won't.
She says she is going to walk out in front of a car, and kill herself.
She walks in the road straight toward an on coming transit van
which nearly hits her.

**homosexual**
There's a train speeding along the railway track.
Stop the train!

Off the train
On the train
Off the train
On the train
Off the train
On the train.
Touch the window.
Open the window.

Off the train
On the train
Off the train
On the train
Off the train
On the train.
Stick your hand against his...
The signal says touch his bum.

## 25th January 2001
## (Rita and Jack)

I have recently discovered something about my girlfriend. Her birth-day, she must have seen him, for definite. She told me she was see-ing someone else on Tuesday. She asked me round for some food to tell me that. She was nice to me before she told me that. She gave me some soup. I remember a long time back, in November; she told me she didn't want to use me for sex. That must have meant she was using someone else for sex. I feel like she was using me to get over her marriage. I feel like she was using me, as a means of sup-port, when she had her breast enlargement. It has made me think you have to use people. That is the only way. You can't leave your-self with nothing. She was seeing me. She was also seeing some-body else. What else did she say? She said that she wanted to be with me. She didn't want to be with anybody else. That was just recently. There was one comment she made about condoms. She talked about me paying for condoms. Perhaps that meant she had paid much for condoms recently. Strange thing is, is that she seems so greedy. I think she wants cock. She wants it badly. Drunk, she is vicious. I am struck, away from the centre. Away from the excite-ment. If I stay sober and work hard, that will be my investment for the future. I will get the upper hand.

Unfortunately, that is how I am measuring life at the moment. Zero money. I don't feel ill anymore. My knee hurts. A lot.

We try and do better work than each other.

The positive side of this is that I can see her and do what I want. How do I know she hasn't done this sort of thing before?

**29.3.01**

My thoughts about staying in my flat were that I was afraid to turn on the electricity. That was because electricity cost money. Money was something I didn't have.

I was up early, worrying. I used the telephone, my mobile, to ring my girlfriend. I knew every second I used that phone cost me money. Before I made the call I had worried myself into a brick wall. I'm always worrying myself into a brick wall.

On the phone we spoke about some of the stuff I'm worrying about. We couldn't talk about all of it. That would be not wise because most of it related to myself and her.

We did, however, talk about how she didn't want to talk about regret. That is very wise not to talk about regret. Why bother.

It is important to understand that it is human to have regrets. You have to have them. You will have them. You have to help yourself deal with them. Basically, you just have to get on. That can be difficult, though.

It is true to say that if you shift yourself from one thing to the other you are in a much stronger position. You find big regrets turn into small regrets. You can make big regrets turn into nothing; big regrets turn into small regrets. That's what I have to do.

## I know i....

I know I've got to write a novel and do it quick because time is running out. I shield lots of stuff, which is a bad thing. The last sentence had nothing to do with the sentence before.

How can I write when I haven't got a printer. I can't print anything out for goodness sake. How comes I try and write this when listening to shit stuff on the cd player.

I don't like using this computer, full stop, because it's not a straightforward typewriter. How can I use this properly when I can do so much with it. Maybe I should forget about the fact that I can do so much with it.

I guess this is proper writing but who is going to publish this shit. Who's going to publish it for fuck sake? And will I, eventually, wear this keyboard out?

Right I'll move swiftly onto dreams. I have not mentioned my dreams in too long a time. I've had two significant dreams recently. The one last night was about people stealing things from me. Two guys in the street decided they should take the spliff I was smoking off me in the street. Which they did. I'd rather give them the spliff than get my head kicked in.

In the other dream, I had a few nights ago; I ended up sharing a house with Samuel Beckett. Big fun.

What I need to do, I think, is not hang out too much with people that don't stretch their creative capabilities. This means I shouldn't be with people who do not do stuff. I should get together with people who do stuff.

**30.3.01 I'm on the train, the 15.34 Blackfriars to Brighton**
I'm thinking to myself, the position I am in isn't too bad. I'm not in a complete mess, concerning finances, although I am poor. I don't think my girlfriend is feeling too good at the moment. When I'm away she'll probably speak to somebody else. I don't mind that. I try not to mind. She has to speak to somebody. Her regrets are getting on top of her.

The good thing about myself is that I know I'll get a chunky wage packet at the end of the month. I have to do something this month to ensure I get a chunky wage packet the following month. At the moment I am resting. I am on holiday.

## 26th October 2001

This morning I woke up, generally in the wrong frame of mind. I mean things were going wrong, wrong for me.

Last night I said to her she was pretty and sexy.

And she kept saying to me, 'you are cooler than anyone else,' 'you are the dogs bollocks.' 'You are cooler than him.'

Why does she keep saying that sort of stuff?

**Tuesday 30th October 2001**

Last night I went to bed at 8pm, so early because I was knackered. I woke up at 2am. I got up. Used the toilet. Made myself a drink. Strangely the lights had been left on from the previous evening and the fire, in the living room. Billy's light was on in his room, as well. I found out the following morning, from John next door, that Billy had collapsed outside the pub, at 10pm. He had been taken to the hospital.

**2nd November 2001**

The truth is my friggin leg is killing me. That is the truth. And I feel like shit. Yesterday morning I felt okay. Today I feel like shit. I don't why that is. I keep thinking too much about work. Whereas I should be thinking about my own work. With what I'm doing I don't have to push myself to a certain point. Wish I had to because at each certain point you get injected with confidence. It is true that I am massively broke, now. I have very little money to last me until November 20th. And it is getting colder.

## The bed

Nothing around.
Neat and tidy.
Few things neat and tidy.
One photograph on the shelf.
The bed. Stuff cluttered around.
Two t.v.'s. Books. Mess. Mess.

The curtains are open.
The window is open.
The sun glares; a thin layer of grey cloud in the sky;
Grey turned golden.
The curtains are pink.
Activity in the street early on a Sunday morning.
8.35 am.
Bang. Bang. Scrape.
Sound of frequent passing car.
Cars sound remotely like the sea.
I draw on my hand
Fall asleep
Wake up
Motorbikes scream past.

**Burgess Park**
I sit here in the blazing sun.
In front of me there are trees, grass and a tower block.
I'm working out who I am.
Inside of my mind I lift my shirt
Collars and call
Myself a writer.

**poem**

Haven't got any money.
I've got no money.

I've got no computer, it's broke,
So is my cd player.

I'll have to stop in.
Although, things are so bad
Staying in won't make any difference
To the debt I'm in.

## 16th February

I woke up knowing that I am going to be broke for another month. My flat mate is playing his music very loud, next door. I don't mind that too much. Sometimes he needs to get what he needs to get out of his system. He'd do this by playing loud music, I think. It is 9.20a.m, Saturday morning. It is a bit early for that sort of thing.

I just fell asleep. I've woken up again one and a half hours later. I still feel broke. I know that I haven't got any money, apart from what I need for food. I'm still in bed. I'll get up in a minute to make myself some breakfast. It's cold. I'm lying low. The walls are a nasty beige, cream colour. They need to be painted. I don't know what colour to paint them. Maybe, I should paint them yellow.

That is the only colour I can clearly visualise.

I'm forcing myself not to watch the t.v.

I lost a notebook. I won't get it back.

Someone is taking me to see a film tonight.

**The two girls and the boy**

The boy, with his shaved black head, walked past the window.

"There he goes, that's him," she said.

"No," the other one said.

"Yeah, that's him, he walks past here at the same time every day. He's all right. Ask him out."

"How? I don't know how to, or when to."

"Lets sort it out."

The two of them had a deep discussion about what to do. The pair of them were just seventeen, the same age as him. They all went to the same college, but didn't know.

"Right, tomorrow," Emma said.

"I can't do it tomorrow. I need time to get myself right."

"You're as right as you will ever be."

So, the next day, they went ahead with Emma's plan.

Emma stood with her bike against a wall. It had a flat tyre. Rachel stood at the end of the street. The end the boy would walk towards. The time was ten to four, the time the boy would walk past the window. Rachel started walking. She walked past the bend and the boy was visible.

Emma had bumped the bike into him, deliberately. She had spent a minute holding him there until Rachel turned up.

"Hi! Rachel." Emma said with enthusiasm, so as to make Rachel look good.

"Hi." Rachel said.

"Oh," Emma said to Paul, "this is my mate Rachel. What's your name?"

"My name is Paul." He said.

"Do you want to go out with each other?"

They both nodded. Emma walked away and left them on their own. She took her bike with her.

## 10th April 2002

It is the 10th April 2002. I have no money left to spend. There are ten days left to pay day. Not sure, exactly what to do. I know that I have Saturday, Sunday and Monday off work next week. That works to my benefit. I think that, maybe definitely, I should take my bike in to sell. If I get, maybe £20.00 for it, then I could buy a hoover bag. I am surrounded, generally, by people who are doing well. I think I'll never see her again in my life. That is sad.

I am writing because I know that I have to continue to fill this note-book. That is the only reason I am continuing to write. I went out today on my bike, to the shop where you can sell items. I didn't in actual fact, sell anything. The guy in the shop, who gets lonely, told me, no, he didn't want to buy what I had to sell. I wanted to sell my bike. It wasn't new enough, apparently. He already had at least one hundred old bikes in the cellar. All of which were waiting for a sale. He was only buying brand new bikes. This was a shame because I needed the cash to buy a hoover bag; the carpet in our flat needed hoovering. So, the hoover bag will have to wait and so will I, for cash. I have none. It doesn't look as though I will get any, for a long time. This is what is killing me, this waiting around. What helps me, a great deal, is getting a job in a bookshop.

I've recently got involved in a job on a magazine that a man is attempting to lift off the ground. Unfortunately, I don't want to get involved with it. Although, if it means getting my story published, it would be worth it.

Trouble I'm faced with is that I have no money and I have no com-puter. I have to do everything by hand, which is an inconvenience. When that lad came into the office he caused quite a stir. Quite a big stir. Then he went. He spent the rest of his life

I need to send that script off. I need to get a computer. I badly need to get a computer, I think. I've got to keep writing those bloody scripts and stop worrying about the money.

What annoys me is that there are those groups of people who have other friends; they look forward to going home to see them. They drive around in Fiat cars and ride bikes with huge carts on the back, or rather, huge trailers. Those bikes are pretty cool, definitely. It helps to do what I am doing now, which is writing.

I should definitely do this more often. I wonder what will happen next in my life. I wonder. It is good I didn't get that driving work, although what I need to do is get some other paid work.

## Poet

Poet feels dead.

**Bridge Lights**
I saw my lover
Before the Chelsea Bridge lights
She stood
In front of me.
She was striking and fresh faced.
She had bobbed hair and a smooth complexion.
In the dark, there at that moment, she moved out of sight
Behind the stairway of a building
Where she'd peep out occasionally.
I began sketching the start of this, barely able to see
In a tatty, small notebook.

We worked in a department store and caught night buses together.
i remember one time walking part of the way, home after saying
bye, on the bus.
it was pouring down.
i got soaked.
i jumped in a black cab after fifteen minutes or so.
I don't remember what time of year it was.

**black cat Frank**
We saw black cat Frank in the garden
Wearing a yellow collar
Walking around slowly.
That was two days before he was found dead.
Dead. Under a parked car.
Dead. Removed. Left in a bin bag outside the front door.
Dead. There.
Not moving. Still.
The body to be buried in the garden where we saw him.

**broke**

Like a broke writer I'm broke.
I'm broke with a bad head.
With a headache I'm broke.
I'm broke in the middle of the night.
Reading, I'm broke,
Writing, I'm broke,
With a girlfriend I'm broke.
In the middle of the night in February, I'm broke, reading stuff and
writing stuff and waiting for the day when I'm not so broke.

i wonder why i couldn't write here before. very strange. i do feel like a bit of a geek doing this but, you know, that is life, i guess. i'm just doing it i guess. I spoke to Rachel on the phone.

### girl downstairs in rain with her friends

Chris. Chris. Come down 'ere. Come down will ya.
What ya ya. I hear from the balcony.
Her and her two friends have a big umbrella in the rain.
Come round my 'ouse in ten minutes, she said.

**I had a girlfriend**
I had a girlfriend.
she says to me I don't love you anymore.
every time she's drunk she'll ring me and
I'll invite her round
or she'll invite herself around after drinking
cocktails in a cocktail bar
or beers in a pub.

**What is the weekend for**
I hate Fridays.
I hate weekends.
That's why I work them.
I mean I go into a workplace and work them.
That is because I don't like them.

Today, Friday, I've heard people on different radio stations mention the weekend.

**Falling**

You find yourself facing the world.
You have a go.
Sometimes you fall.
You get struck by one thing or the other.
You get wounded.

You keep going.
You do what you can.
You do what you can for a long time.
Eventually you are flattened.
You are flattened into a pancake.

You are a pancake for so long you accept that that is the way it is.
It's called being flattened by a long slog.

**coffee stained notebook**
It is 1 am January the first, 2002.
I celebrated New Year by watching a big t.v.
With my girl No.1.
I'm stoned.
I'm drinking whiskey in an armchair.

## 22nd June 2002

There isn't really much point in writing the date above as it has no significance to what I'm writing. It does label this as some kind of diary, which it isn't. The problem is always waiting for the right moment to do this. There never will be the right moment. I could end up waiting around forever if I'm not careful.

What I thought of writing in the shower was that I always feel unhappy about something. I know in the past I have felt unhappier than this. That is the truth. I, generally, will always feel unhappy, but I'm sure something could happen to make me feel happy. Why stop here? There is no good answer to that except that I know I'll write nothing of any use, if I carry on. Could there be a certain elegance about scatty writing? I doubt that.

Pure writing. None of that stuff. I know that she'll require a certain degree of backing whilst she is going through her dry patch. I have gone through a dry patch before. I wasn't all that pleasant. I have definitely, very much, got to get my head into this and keep going. I have to do that. How comes I'm struggling for money again. I don't know the answer to that. This problem will go on and on and on. Whilst I was studying I took a break from everything. That is something a person shouldn't do even if they want to become a great writer.

**The Writer's Telephone Answering Machine**
I went to the top of the stairs.
I looked down through the gap
Between the stairs and the ceiling.
I looked at the answering machine.
The red light was not flashing.
There were no messages.

**The Girl with the Pink Top in the Café**
She reads Harry Potter.

She has a blue bra strap.

She has red nail varnish. Long brown hair and dark skin. As she eats her brown bap, she looks down at the table self-consciously. When she finishes eating her bap she rubs her hands together. Then she puts her handbag strap around her shoulder. She stands up, walks to the back of the café and orders a hot apple pie.

**Demolish**
Break. Get rid of. Pull down.
Thoughts crashing through my head.
Vandalism. Vandal.
Vandal. Vandal. Break. Break.

**Distraught**

Today I feel completely useless,
Completely distraught.

But that is how a poet should feel, isn't it?
Wrecked, hungry, lonely.

### end of March

Glass smashes on the plate.
Smash.
An odd piece of glass
Lies on the floor.

(The fork rattled and the glass smashed).

**Wired up**

I've got the best and right artist working with me that I could ever imagine having.

I've got a great typographer working with me, the best I can imagine having.

I like my publisher.

My mate came round this afternoon. He has tattoos on his arms. He went to the chippy and got some chips, which he brought back. We ate them, then I had to go sharpish. I had to meet up with another mate. We walked down the road and spoke about this poem, Wired Up. I told him I'd changed the title three times. I had some trouble with my leg and was using a crutch, so at the bus stop, he helped me pull in the bus.

When I met my other mate we walked down near Cork Street, where he found a tenner in the roadside.

## 2nd June 2003

It used to be that whenever I wrote stuff, it made me feel better. It had a cathartic effect, whatever that means. Now, I'm standing here at London Bridge 9.26 one early summer evening, using a pen from Woolworth's and I'm wondering will writing ever have that effect again.

I'm getting a train to my girlfriend's house. She'll be there after a long night out with her friends at a work leaving party; she had a good time and I asked her too much on the phone. What time did you get in? Not too late, she'd reply. It was after 5 o'clock (they'd always be out, until at least that time, the three of them). Can you believe it, though, while they were still up taking drugs, probably winding down, I was getting up for work. I had a long day. We were short staffed and had to make a lot of money.

## Nothing

I've got nothing
Absolutely nothing.
If I had something
Life would be a lot easier.

**old poem**

I like her because she prefers walking through sixties housing estates to going to expensive restaurants.

**the couch**

He went to a seaside town
to talk things through
with his ex-girlfriend.
She looked beautiful,
more beautiful than ever and more
beautiful than anyone he knew.
She said she hadn't watched t.v.
for a while, whilst
they were sitting watching it in silence.
They went to the pub,
sat in near silence and
had two half pints, each.

**public places**
Toilets.
Cinemas.
Back gardens.
Cars in the day when it's raining.

**poem**

If you make mistakes,

That's mistakes made.

After, accept you made them and get on with life.

Don't walk around with your head down thinking I've done this,
I've done that.

The key to being successful is not to be bothered about being successful.

**museum**

I walked along the river with that girl, yesterday.
It was winter.
The sun shone. She wanted to go and see the Tate. The old Tate.
Instead of that we went into the gardening history museum.
After, we walked to my place. On the way she asked me how I'd
like to be buried.

**Looking Forward to**

Looking forward to going to my flat.

Looking forward to seeing my friends all over London.

Looking forward to checking my post.

Looking forward to checking my landline telephone messages.

Looking forward to my knee fixing itself.

Looking forward to borrowing £100.00 from the bank to see me through to the next month.

Looking forward to drinking wine.

Looking forward to eating food.

Looking forward to.

nnnnnnnnnnnnnnnnnnnnnnnnnnnnnnnnnnnnnnnnnnnnnnnnnnnnnnnnnnnnn
nnnnnnnnnnnnnnnnnnnnnnnnnnnnnnn

**blizzard**
one Saturday night I watched t.v. in my room.
The curtains were open so you could see the streetlights outside.
On a sudden moment I noticed dark blobs dancing on the wall
behind the television.
They were shadows;
shadows from the streetlights and the snowflakes.

## post blues

Post bla bla blues.
Post bla BLA blues.
Post bla bla blues.

**making it today**
I've made it.
I haven't made it.
I've made it.
I haven't made it.

**cold pizza part one**
This is not a romantic poem.

I got in last night from work.
I established I had worked thirteen days back to back.
I fell asleep at 7.30pm. I woke up at 10.
I went downstairs to watch t.v. with my flat mates.
They went to bed before me.
I went up at 12. I switched the t.v. and lights off.
I fell asleep, not straight away, but soon.
I woke up at 8am. Got up. Went back to bed. Woke up again at
10.30am. I went out after having just one cup of tea. I went to
Iceland, bought pizzas, baked beans.

**cold pizza part two**
This is a romantic poem.

On the way home
I saw Ûlku in the local supermarket.

She gave me grapes, a newspaper, for free.
When I went in there again she gave me the right biscuits to buy.
Later I eat a pizza, cheese and tomato. Some is left, cold.

## my legs
My friggin legs hurt.
My legs hurt so bad.
I'm dying.
Yes I am.

**thumb**

My thumb poem would have been perfect
Had I written it in the
Pub all that time ago.
All that week ago
I sat on my own waiting
For her, looking at my
Thumb.
I wrote the title and that was it.
I'm starting all over again.
Thumb.
My thumb I see in front of trees;
In front of a green lawn and a sign saying,
'Please keep off the grass.'
I see it and smell the perfume of flowers.
I see it and listen to the birds singing. I'm in the Chelsea
Physic gardens.
I see it in front of the back of elegantly shaped Chelsea buildings.
My thumb is crinkled in the middle.
I can bend it.
The nail is square.
The more I look at it, the more it looks like it's not mine.

**The Elephant and Castle Shopping Centre**
One of the great designs of the fifties,
Now a sophisticated block;
I'd go in there and admire it's soft inner edges
The delicate curves
The inner splendour.
I'd spend long afternoons
Watching, writing prose, sipping coffee
Listening to quiet, crisp echoes.

there is a hat stall at the bottom of the escalators.
the hats have strong, bright colours.
(the bookshop is on the same floor).

**food and drink**

Today, at 4.40, I went to the shop.

It was just getting dark.

'Cheques cashed', 'Coral', 'Allied Carpets', 'Costcutter'.

I went into Costcutter.

I picked up one bottle of Volvic water

and some food.

I went to the counter.

Two people were in front of me. The first person bought Strongbow. She had a black, three quarter length, shiny coat on.

The next person to get served bought food and a small bottle of gin.

**November night**

Thirty minutes past midnight. Sunday night I walk home, on
Clapham High Street, from the bus stop. A girl approaches me.
She has a black coat on. Brown dirty hair. She holds a cigarette,
barely the butt
Remaining. Her finger nails are dirty.

"Excuse me.
Can you give me some money for my train fare home?"
She forces tears to flood out of her eyes,
To soak her cheeks.
She sobs.
"It's my birthday. I've been dumped. Can you give me a cuddle?"

This was all thrown at me within a few moments. I wanted to give
her a cuddle, but was scared she might put her hands in my pock-
ets and steal my money.
Or else, although she looked so frail, she could have pierced me
with a sharp knife.

I held her hands.
I asked her name. Her name was Chloe. She wanted to go to a town
maybe 30 miles away.

She asked if I was walking in 'that direction.' I said yes.
We walked. She asked if I had any money. I said, no.

Another man walked by.
Have you got any money, she said. He said, no.
She left me to walk on. I glanced back
again
and again
until she went out of sight.

**Write**

I've got nothing playing on the t.v.
I've got no music playing.

I'm sitting here, stoned.
it's 8 o'clock pm.
it's getting dark.

I thought about what to write before I got this pen on the paper.
what I thought to write I haven't.

**confidence**

When someone is nasty to you and your confidence gets blown to shreds, you think to yourself, did you ever, at some stage, do that to somebody else.

**penniless**
me, penniless.
now I remember that we could fight and she could stand it. The fighting. She took part in it.
This is the garden that I meant. This is it, the garden that I meant. She shows me a picture of it. She reads about gardens. I want her. I am tall. She is cute, short. Red hair, crooked mouth.

### Rotten

Feeling rotten because I'm running low
On what is called money.
I need some
Very badly.
I keep having to pay out lots of money
All the time.

**untitled 20/03/02**

I woke up this morning in a terrible mood. It must have something to do with the bad weather. The winter is going on and on and on. The winter is going on.

I'm thinking that there isn't anything to look forward to when the winter is over. There'll be more misery in the sunshine.

**My Mum and Dad**
Must be intrigued to
See what happens in
My life; they paid
Special interest when
I told them I might
Have children at aged 34.
They said, well he did
That and that at that age,
That's when they had
Children and they turned
Out well and all
Nice things.

**Rita said to Jack**
Tonight she said to me:
I feel depressed.
I feel like killing myself.
I feel like throwing myself under a bus.

**pregnancy**

Our friendship has lasted a long time.

You're at an age, now, when you want a child.

I can't do that for you.

Sometimes we talk and talk and talk.

I like it when you talk about Paris, Barthes and semiotics.

You talk about other stuff as well; mostly design.

I like the way you daydream. Once I met you at the tube station

And watched you when you didn't know I was looking.

That time you were fixated, staring at a dog. Other times you might stare at a leaf or a cloud. This behaviour that you also induce in me, helps me to stop getting preoccupied with what I shouldn't be preoccupied with.

That will have to end now. We can't see each anymore because I've met someone else. She doesn't want me to see you, probably, because I told her that you told me that you didn't want her to go to your thirtieth birthday party.

I can't do it. I can't get you pregnant.

You should meet someone else, as well. Preferably not someone who has a bad drug habit.

**Rut**

People get stuck in ruts.
They can't afford holidays.
They don't have breaks.
They stuck in same state, or way of being.

### Sleeping woman

She had her pyjamas on.
The top, the t-shirt, did not match the bottoms.

It was 7am.
She lay under the covers
By the wall facing it.
She was curled up.
Her bum faced me.
She was half asleep.

Her soft toy rat was in the bed,
Billy.
I made him walk across the covers toward her.
He sniffed her and
Nibbled her.
She giggled.

She grabbed hold of him
And held him between her
Upper arm and body.
She fell back to sleep.

**small t.v.**

i've got a small t.v.
I want a big one.
The picture's bad unless the aerial is twisted right.
My video is big: it's twenty years old, at least.
I've got a DVD player.

**Blue Eye Song**
Don't
Need morphine
To say you've got beautiful eyes.

You wore a stripy t-shirt
When I was in recovery.
When I saw you I saw
Your piercing blue eyes

But I don't need morphine
To tell you how beautiful they are.

**Scar Wall**
In a fit of anger
I hurled my wine glass of beer
Against the wall.
It splattered into tiny pieces
And the beer, the half glass full, disappeared into the air.
The next day I noticed a piece of glass
Stuck in the wall, which I removed.
It had left a scar
The shape of a smile
As long as the width of a mobile phone.

## Ms Splendid

I love you more than Mrs Cloghead. I've wanted to tell you I love you.

I got a taxi back to my flat tonight. The taxi driver said, "look after yourself." I think he said that. It was nice whatever he said.

I opened the side gate to my front door and felt this awful empty feeling. I still feel that. I'm in from that Sunday evening wind blowing. Why had I felt that emptiness? It is going now. I'm laying in bed listening to loud music, which will sleep off in twenty five minutes.

The occasional aeroplane flies past. It roars, cutting through the black sky.

Darkness is about. My head is cloudy dark.

What did we talk about today? I'm willing to get violent on paper. Some agreement. Some talk. You didn't want to talk about politics. You said you didn't care.

After, you mentioned couch, settee, sofa and living room, front room and lounge. Then you said scone or scon. You like talking about all this stuff.

It's in your head and suddenly you want to talk about it, nurse Splendid, head of the hotel. Maker, provider of toast.